W9-ACM-867

ORGAN & BODY

DONATION

Essential Viewpoints

ORGAN & BODY

DONATION

BY HAL MARCOVITZ

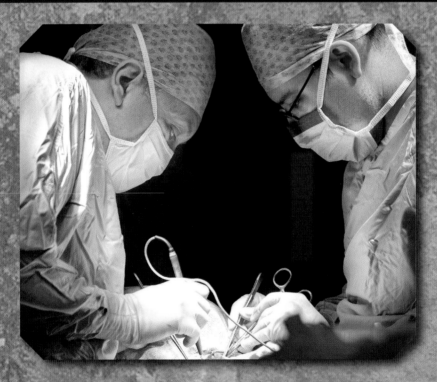

Content Consultant
Tamar Klaiman, Research Assistant Professor
Georgetown University, O'Neill Institute
for National and Global Health Law

ABDO
Publishing Company

CREDITS

Published by ABDO Publishing Company, 8000 West 78th Street, Edina, Minnesota 55439. Copyright © 2011 by Abdo Consulting Group, Inc. International copyrights reserved in all countries. No part of this book may be reproduced in any form without written permission from the publisher. The Essential Library™ is a trademark and logo of ABDO Publishing Company.

Printed in the United States of America,
North Mankato, Minnesota
052010
092010

 THIS BOOK CONTAINS AT LEAST 10% RECYCLED MATERIALS.

Editor: Amy Van Zee
Copy Editor: Paula Lewis
Interior Design and Production: Kazuko Collins
Cover Design: Kazuko Collins

Library of Congress Cataloging-in-Publication Data
Marcovitz, Hal.
  Organ and body donation / Hal Marcovitz.
      p. cm. — (Essential viewpoints)
  Includes bibliographical references and index.
  ISBN 978-1-61613-524-9
  1. Donation of organs, tissues, etc.—Juvenile literature. I. Title.
  RD129.5.M36 2011
  617.9′5—dc22

                            2010002656

TABLE OF CONTENTS

*Chris Klug competed as a snowboarder in the 2002
Winter Olympics in Salt Lake City, Utah.*

OVERCOMING
THE ODDS

Twenty-nine-year-old snowboarder Chris
Klug was about to compete in the final run
for a bronze medal at the 2002 Winter Olympics
in Salt Lake City, Utah. First, he had to overcome a
minor equipment problem that could have ruined

his run down the mountain. On Klug's previous run, the buckle on his boot snapped off, costing him a measure of control.

With just seconds to go, Klug and some friends made a quick repair. They used duct tape and a piece of scrap metal to hold his boot together. With his boot repaired, Klug glided down the mountain in the men's parallel giant slalom event, easily beating Nicolas Huet of France to take the bronze. Following the race, Klug compared the broken boot buckle to some of the other problems he has overcome. "I've faced worse odds before," Klug said.[1]

Two years earlier, his liver was failing. He suffered from a rare disease, primary sclerosing cholangitis (PSC), which blocks the bile ducts in the organ. For nine years, the disease had caused Klug's liver to deteriorate. By the summer of 2000, he was in critical condition. A liver transplant saved his life.

ACCIDENTAL SHOOTING

In July 2000, Leisa Flood left her home in suburban Denver, Colorado, to run an errand. She was gone for no more than 15 minutes. But when she arrived home, she found her 13-year-old son Billy collapsed on the sofa. He had been accidentally shot in the head. Doctors tried to save his life, keeping Billy alive with the help of a machine that kept his blood pumping. After three days, Flood was told there was no hope. She was asked to donate Billy's organs.

Approximately 200 miles (322 km) across the state, Klug was living in Aspen and patiently waiting for a liver to become available for transplant. For months, his condition worsened. He had grown weak and was enduring bouts of high fever, vomiting, loss of appetite, and muscle and joint aches.

Located on the right side of the upper abdomen, the liver is a vital organ. It stores

PSC and Walter Payton

The disease that afflicted Chris Klug also afflicted Walter Payton, who is regarded as one of the best halfbacks to have ever played football. In 1999, Payton disclosed that he suffered from PSC and was in need of a liver transplant. Bile was building up and damaging his liver cells. He was placed on the waiting list for a liver. But within weeks, doctors discovered the disease had progressed into cancer in his bile ducts. He died nine months after his diagnosis.

Payton wrote that initially he felt confident a donor would be found. However, he soon learned that was not necessarily the case. "When I first heard that I would die if they couldn't get me a liver within two years, I thought no problem," he said, "but then I found out the odds might not be so good. And it doesn't make any sense. If everyone agreed to organ donation, there wouldn't be any list at all."[2] While that may not be entirely true, the wait for organs would be much shorter, and more lives could be saved.

vitamins, sugars, and fats, which it then uses to manufacture important proteins. The liver also produces bile, which enables digestion, and it breaks down and neutralizes harmful substances, such as alcohol. Klug's liver functions were failing as his disease progressed.

Suddenly, a pager hooked to Klug's belt started beeping. It meant a donor had been found. Klug hurried to University Hospital in Denver, where Billy's liver was transplanted into Klug's body.

Making the Decision

When doctors told Leisa Flood that her son would not recover from a gunshot wound, she had to decide whether to donate his organs. "I was thinking, 'Oh, they're going to cut my boy up in little pieces.' But then, I was just sitting with him and thinking about what a giving and loving person he was. He would want someone to live."[3]

GRAVESIDE VISIT

Generally, donors and recipients are unknown to each other, but with permission, the organ donation organizers gave Klug's name to Flood. She wept when she learned that her son's liver had been donated to an Olympic snowboarder. Since the Floods moved to Colorado, Billy had become enamored with winter sports in the mountainous state, particularly snowboarding. But Flood, a single mother, could not afford to buy her son a board.

Billy owned a snowboarding video game, though, which he played enthusiastically.

Klug had been in excellent shape before the surgery and recovered quickly. He left the hospital just four days after receiving the new liver. At first, Klug limited his exercise to long walks, but he gradually built up his strength. Within a few weeks, he started lifting weights and jogging. A few months after the procedure, Klug returned to competitive snowboarding.

As Klug prepared to compete in the Olympics, Flood visited her son's grave. She told Billy he was going to the Olympics.

URGENT NEED

Each year, between 20,000 and 30,000 organs are transplanted in U.S. hospitals. The number of transplanted organs has increased steadily over the years. In the late 1980s, fewer than 13,000 organs were transplanted yearly. The increase is due in part

An Ambassador for Organ Transplant

Since receiving his new liver, Chris Klug has served as an ambassador for the cause of organ donation. He makes several speeches each year to help raise awareness about the need for organs. He even started the Chris Klug Foundation to "promote lifesaving donation and improve quality of life for donors, donor families, organ transplant candidates and recipients."[4]

The kidney is a commonly transplanted organ because the donor can be living.

to better medical techniques. In addition, people are more aware of organ transplantation. In many states today, people can sign up to be organ donors when they apply for driver's licenses.

Still, the number of people waiting for organ donations far exceeds the number of organs available for transplant. According to the U.S. Health Resources and Services Administration, some 100,000 people are waiting for new hearts, livers, lungs, kidneys, and other body parts.

While the vast majority of organs are harvested from nonliving donors, organs can also be taken from live donors. Each year, approximately 6,000 live donors provide their organs. These are mostly kidneys, as the human body contains two kidneys and can function with just one. Sometimes, surgeons can also remove pieces of other organs from a living donor. This occurs most often when a portion of an adult's liver is transplanted into a child. The transplanted piece of liver will grow with the child.

THE HEART OF THE CONTROVERSY

Often, the main roadblock that stands between patients and new organs stems from a hazy definition of death. All 50 states, as well as the District of Columbia, regard death as the moment when the heart or brain ceases to function. However, medical advances have made it possible to

Live Liver Donors

It is possible for a live donor to provide part of his or her liver. Because of the liver's power to regenerate new cells, partial livers can grow into full-size, healthy livers within weeks of surgery. In 2003, Keith Karzin of Valencia, California, donated a portion of his liver to his mother-in-law, Sharon Dziubala. Both recovered. "My wife and I talked about it and went to my mother-in-law, but [my in-laws] didn't want me to do it," Karzin said. "They were really concerned because I have three young kids and they didn't want anything to happen. My attitude was, 'Nothing's going to happen. This is going to be good. This was meant to be.'"[5]

keep people alive artificially after their brains or hearts have stopped working. This was the case in Billy Flood's death. As doctors struggle to define the moment of death, they or the deceased's loved ones are often hesitant to proceed with organ removal surgery. Many fear removing organs from people who could be revived.

Other moral and ethical issues surface as well. Although most major religions consider organ donation a charitable act, some religious people refuse to donate their organs or accept organs provided by others.

Meanwhile, the business of obtaining whole bodies for scientific research—a trade dishonored by past inappropriate practices—hit new lows in recent years. Investigators uncovered several cases in which employees associated with cadaver donation programs were found to be selling bodies and body parts on a black market. One of the recipients of the illegal body parts was the U.S. Army. The army uses body parts to

Leonardo da Vinci and Grave Robbing

Using dead bodies to learn about how the body works is not a new practice. Leonardo da Vinci, who lived from 1452 to 1519, was a famous artist, scientist, and inventor. During his lifetime, the scientific details of the body were unknown. In order to study human anatomy, Leonardo most likely took corpses from graves. As a result, he drew some of the first accurate renderings of the human body.

test armor issued to soldiers who may be exposed to land mine explosions. However, cadavers may also be used to teach students, particularly medical students, about how the body works.

There is a long waiting list for organs in the United States. Currently, it is illegal in all but a handful of countries to pay someone to provide an organ. However, some patients desperate for kidneys have found impoverished people in other countries who are willing to sell their organs. There is an active trade in organs in India, South America, and other developing areas. Because of this organ trade, some physicians and bioethicists have called for laws permitting people in the United States and elsewhere to be paid for their kidneys, too.

As physicians, bioethicists, attorneys, lawmakers, and others work to resolve these issues, organ transplant hopefuls wait for organs to become available. Most patients are fully aware of the deadlines under which they live. Says Klug, "To receive the gift of life is a humbling experience. . . . I will forever be grateful for my second chance."[6]

Today, Chris Klug is a strong supporter of organ donation.

Chapter 2

An 1830 portrait of Mary Wollstonecraft Shelley, author of Frankenstein

HISTORY OF DONATION

Organ transplantation did not become widely accepted in the medical community until the 1950s. Evidence suggests, however, that doctors have contemplated over the medical benefits of transplants for hundreds, if not thousands, of years. Well-meaning, but largely ignorant, physicians of ancient times likely tried their hands at the practice. However, they did not possess the surgical skills or the scientific knowledge necessary to conduct the surgeries. Accounts also tell of doctors transplanting the hearts of dead warriors into the chests of so-called cowards, supposedly to give their patients the bravery they lacked.

Other ancient documents chronicle humankind's curiosity about transplantation. These texts discuss skin transplants done by Hindus in India around 3000 BCE. Hua-Tuo was a Chinese surgeon around the year 200 CE. He performed many surgeries, including the removal of the spleen. He speculated on the value of using donated organs to replace the diseased organs of his patients.

ORGANS FROM CADAVERS

During the seventeenth, eighteenth, and nineteenth centuries, many doctors and scientists made successful skin grafts and similar minor surgeries. Although the concept of organ transplantation was still in its infancy, some visionaries could see tremendous potential. In 1816, Mary Wollstonecraft Shelley wrote the novel

Frankenstein. The book is a science fiction classic. Its teenage author proved to be remarkably farsighted when she predicted that organs could be removed from cadavers and used to sustain life.

Meanwhile, physicians were refining their surgical techniques. After decades of experiments on animals, they started making successful human organ and tissue transplants. On December 7, 1905, Austrian ophthalmologist Eduard Zirm performed the first successful human transplant—

Mary Wollstonecraft Shelley

The wife of poet Percy Shelley, Mary Wollstonecraft Shelley was 18 years old in the summer of 1816. The Shelleys shared a villa on the shores of Lake Geneva in Switzerland with their friend, the poet Lord George Gordon Byron. As a game, Byron challenged the others to write scary stories. Mary wrote *Frankenstein*.

Mary Shelley said a nightmare inspired her to write the book. She had dreamed of dead bodies returning to life. "Perhaps the component parts of a creature might be manufactured, brought together, and endued with vital warmth," she later remarked.[1]

Frankenstein is the story of physician Victor Frankenstein, who reconstructs a human body by using organs and other parts he harvested from cadavers. "The dissecting room and the slaughter-house furnished many of my materials; and often did my human nature turn with loathing from my occupation," Victor relates in the novel.[2]

In the era in which Mary Wollstonecraft Shelley wrote the novel, the science of transplanting organs was still in its infancy. Eventually, physicians determined that organs remained viable in a cadaver for no more than 30 minutes after the heart stops beating due to the loss of nutrients provided by circulating blood.

---

the cornea of an eye. The first successful kidney transplant was performed in 1954. In 1963, the first liver and lung transplants were performed. By the 1960s, doctors had discovered that the major impediment to a successful transplant was the body's rejection of the new organ. The recipient's immune system would treat the organ as a hostile foreign object and fight it. If the donor and recipient were closely related, the recipient's immune system might accept the organ. Until then, most of the donors had been close genetic matches to the recipients, such as siblings or other relatives. This was the era in which antirejection drugs were developed, although they would not become effective until the 1980s.

First Heart Transplant

On December 2, 1967, a young South African woman named Denise Darvall was hit by a car while crossing a street in the city of Cape Town. She was declared brain-dead, although her heart continued to beat. Meanwhile, grocery store owner Louis Washkansky had been admitted to a Cape Town hospital with severe heart disease. Local surgeon Christiaan Barnard performed the world's first heart transplant one day after Darvall's accident.

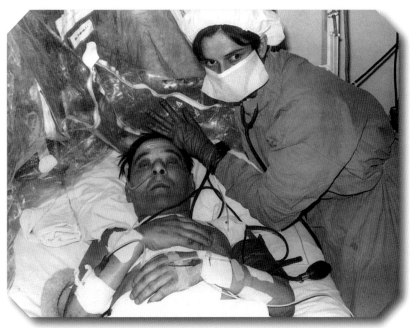

*Louis Washkansky was the first heart transplant recipient.
He underwent surgery at the Groote Schuur Hospital
in Cape Town, South Africa, in 1967.*

Barnard, as well as surgeons in other countries,
had been preparing for this moment for years.
They had experimented on animals and refined the
techniques they would need to perform the surgery
on human patients. They came to believe that the
heart could be transplanted given its relatively simple
mechanics. In essence, the heart is a pump that
circulates blood, providing nutrients to the body.
Later, Barnard described the history-making surgery
he had performed:

As soon as the donor died, we opened her chest and connected her to a heart-lung machine, suffusing her body so that we could keep the heart alive. I cut out the heart. We examined it, and as soon as we found it was normal, we put it in a dish containing solution at 10 degrees centigrade to cool it down further.

We then transferred this heart to the operating room where we had the patient and we connected it to the heart-lung machine. From the time we cut out the heart it was four minutes until we had oxygenated blood going back to the heart muscle from the donor's heart-lung machine. We then excised the patient's heart.[3]

It took Barnard and his team just two hours to transplant the young woman's heart into the man's body. The heart is the easiest organ to transplant because it primarily requires reattaching four blood vessels. Other organ transplants

The Heart of Clive Haupt

A month after Christiaan Barnard performed the first heart transplant on Louis Washkansky, he performed the procedure again on Philip Blaiberg, a Cape Town dentist. Blaiberg survived for 19 months.

The transplant became a political breakthrough as well as a medical breakthrough. The donor, Clive Haupt, was a South African of multiracial ethnicity. During the era of apartheid in South Africa, the news that the heart of a multiracial man had been transplanted into the body of a white patient sparked international headlines. A journalist for *Ebony* magazine wrote, "Clive Haupt's heart will ride in the uncrowded train coaches marked 'For Whites Only' instead of in the crowded ones reserved for blacks. . . . It will enter fine restaurants, attend theaters and concerts and live in a decent home instead of in the tough slums where Haupt grew up."[4]

**The Anatomy
Act of 1832**

It was not until 1832 that authorities in Great Britain recognized that medical students needed a legal provision for bodies to dissect. Until then, medical schools had relied mostly on bodies of executed criminals. In 1832, the British parliament adopted the Anatomy Act. This made it legal for doctors to dissect bodies donated by family members. It helped medical schools train student doctors, and it stopped the illegal practice of snatching bodies from newly dug graves.

involve reattaching many more blood vessels. A day after the surgery, Washkansky sat up in bed and talked with his doctor and family members. Eleven days after the surgery, he took a walk around the hospital floor. Washkansky's story is remarkable, but it does not have a happy ending. Washkansky died 18 days after the surgery. At the time, drugs to fight rejection of the organ had still not been fully developed. His immune system broke down, and he died of pneumonia. Nevertheless, his death led to a greater understanding of the challenges and opportunities of organ transplantation.

Since Washkansky's surgery, antirejection drugs have gone through major developments. Surgical techniques have been refined, and organ transplants have become relatively routine. However, they are still regarded as major surgeries. Today, more than 2,000 people in the United States receive heart transplants each year. Most of these patients go on to lead long, normal lives. For many transplant recipients, their eventual deaths are from causes other than transplanted organ failure.

BODIES FOR SCIENCE

Today's doctors owe a great debt to doctors of centuries past, who endured many hardships as they learned anatomy. Their hard-earned discoveries would lay the groundwork for transplant medicine.

For centuries, many teachers of medicine were unable to find enough cadavers for their students to dissect. In Europe, the Christian church frowned on dissection. Authorities believed such a fate was reserved for the bodies of outcasts, such as criminals, paupers, and those who committed suicide. They believed that good souls deserved a Christian burial.

"Burking" in Scotland

During the early 1800s in Scotland, the medical school at Edinburgh University had a steady supply of bodies due to the efforts of William Burke. Eventually, authorities determined that Burke was not stealing the corpses from graves but killing the victims and selling the bodies to the school. Burke was convicted and hanged. His body was then dissected at the university. Due to Burke's notoriety, this form of murder—killing to sell the corpse—became known as "burking."

The Story of William Hewson

In the 1700s, British physician William Hewson and his students dissected corpses in the basement of a home at 36 Craven Street in London. Hewson died of blood poisoning in 1774 at the age of 34. Historians believe he may have cut himself with a scalpel that carried germs from a cadaver.

These restrictions left medical schools with few bodies to study, so they resorted to illegal methods to obtain cadavers. In one case, English physician William Hewson hired grave robbers to steal corpses. Hewson conducted his anatomy lessons in the basement of a London boarding house.

Attitudes about dissection began to change in the nineteenth century. Today, legal procedures have been established for people who wish to donate their bodies to medical schools. The bodies can also provide tissue to burn patients and organs to patients waiting for transplants. Many people sign living wills, also known as advance directives, providing their bodies to science and transplant patients after their deaths.

Heart transplant surgeon Christiaan Barnard at a press conference in 1967, following the death of Louis Washkansky, his patient

*Organs must be removed from a body soon after death
to be viable for transplant.*

DEFINING DEATH

*A*fter the first heart transplant,
physicians realized the immense
ethical issues they would face as organ transplants
became more successful and more common. They
feared organs might be removed from a person

presumed dead who actually had a chance to live. They realized that a clear definition of death needed to be established and followed by all doctors involved in a transplant.

Establishing a clear and precise definition would be difficult. Some doctors would be hesitant to walk away from their patients until well after their final breaths were drawn. However, transplant doctors need to move quickly. Organs that are not removed or otherwise preserved in the body (through a blood-thinning and chemical-cooling process) lose their viability for transplant within 30 minutes after the heart stops beating.

Uniform Determination of Death

Long ago, doctors used to hold a mirror over a dead person's mouth— if the mirror did not fog from breath, then they knew the patient

Fears of Premature Burial

Throughout history, many people have feared being buried alive. Edgar Allan Poe wrote stories about premature burial in the nineteenth century, and he was horrified that he might face the same fate. In Europe, some tombs were outfitted with electrical devices that enabled the not-quite-deceased to ring bells should they find themselves buried alive. A device that sounded an alarm when it sensed movement in the coffin was patented in the United States in 1983.

was really dead. Even before the introduction of life-support machines, doctors continually fretted that they were giving up on patients who still might recover. And the patients' families and friends wondered the same.

In 1968, soon after Barnard's breakthrough surgery, leaders of the medical community met at Harvard University. They intended to provide a clear definition of death to be employed in transplant cases. Their efforts eventually resulted in the Uniform Determination of Death Act, which

Harvesting Organs from Infants

Some babies are born with anencephaly, which means they are missing large portions of their brains and skulls. Typically, these babies die within days of their births. They are regarded as prime candidates for organ donation.

Due to their extremely delicate nature, organs from deceased infants may have to be harvested within seconds of the moment of death. Even the briefest loss of oxygen may make the organs unusable for transplant. Some transplant activists have argued that organ harvesting procedures from these infants should begin before death has been declared. These procedures may involve injecting drugs that cool the organs. In 1994, the American Medical Association Council on Ethical and Judicial Affairs said that beginning these procedures before death of the anencephalic infant was acceptable, if parental consent is obtained.

However, critics of organ transplant insist that subjecting even anencephalic infants to organ harvesting before the moment of death is inhumane. University of Southern California law professor Alexander Morgan Capron says,

Encouraging [parents] to donate vital organs from their infant will merely intensify their agony or involve them in a decision that they ought not be asked to make: whether one life should be ended to benefit another.[1]

has been adopted by all 50 states and the District of Columbia.

The act says death has occurred when an individual has "sustained either irreversible cessation of circulatory and respiratory functions, or irreversible cessation of all functions of the entire brain."[2] People are considered dead when they can no longer draw breaths and their hearts cease to function, or when their brains stop working.

Since adoption of that standard, medical science has developed tests that can clearly indicate the level of electrical activity in the brain. When electrical activity is absent, the patient is regarded as brain-dead, which is considered dead under the act. Doctors can then remove the organs as long as they have received permission through a living will, organ donor designation on a license or donor card, or from the survivors of the deceased person.

Database of Nondonors

Living wills or advance directives are legal documents that give family members instructions on when to shut off life-sustaining machines should patients become incapacitated. They also leave instructions about organ donation. But many people fail to create living wills. In such a case, the family is in charge of deciding whether an incapacitated person may become an organ donor. They could agree to donate organs despite their loved one's wishes.

DoNotTransplant.com, a group based in California, has taken measures to address this problem. Its online database invites people to register as nondonors. By consulting the database, the group says, family members and hospital officials can ensure that organs are not harvested from patients who do not want to be donors.

WARY OF PHYSICIANS' INTENTIONS

A patient's brain may be functioning, but the heart may have stopped working on its own. In this case, the patient may have suffered cardiac arrest. Machines can take over the work of the lungs and heart, but for how long? Who and what criteria determine when the life-support machines are turned off?

Some critics suggest that doctors, anxious to begin the organ transplant process, are too pushy. They urge families to authorize the end of life-support measures while the patients could still be revived. A few activists have established groups, such as Organ Keeper and DoNotTransplant.com, that warn family members to be wary of physicians' intentions.

In some cases, the heart can restart on its own once the machine has been turned off. After years of study, hospitals have developed a varying range of protocols for ensuring the patient is truly dead once the life support has been

Organ Keeper Cards

People can authorize donation of their organs when they apply for driver's licenses. In most states, the license will include the words "Organ Donor."

For those who do not wish to be organ donors, Organ Keeper, a group based in Middletown, Rhode Island, offers wallet cards that explicitly state the carrier does not wish to be an organ donor.

stopped. Some hospitals approve organ harvesting to commence as early as 75 seconds after the machines are turned off. Others make the surgeons wait as long as five minutes. Because transplant surgeons feel they can wait as long as 30 minutes to begin harvesting organs, waiting five minutes may seem minor, but the issue is complex. As soon as the heart stops pumping blood, the organs begin to deteriorate due to lack of oxygen.

The deterioration can be slowed by injecting drugs that thin the blood and cool the organs. This process slows decay, but it often has to start before the patient clinically dies. This raises the ethical issue of whether doctors have, essentially, begun the harvesting process before death. "This person is not dead yet," insists Jerry A. Menikoff, an associate professor of law, ethics, and medicine at the University of Kansas. "They are going to be dead, but we should be honest and say that we're starting to remove organs a few minutes before they meet the legal definition of death."[3]

Unseemly Procedure

Many doctors insist on waiting longer than 75 seconds or even five minutes after the machines are turned off. As a result, the patient's organs will likely not be usable after doctors declare the patient dead.

Some bioethicists find the entire procedure of harvesting organs to be unseemly. They believe the process largely ignores the grief of the deceased's family. They argue that grieving family members are entitled to time alone with their loved one, even after death. A medical team should not be waiting in the next room, ready to start dissecting a family's loved one. "The image this creates is people hovering over the body trying to get organs any way they can," says Michael A. Grodin, the director of bioethics at Boston University. "There's a kind of macabre flavor to it."[4] However, organ transplant counselors are often called to speak with grieving families and to ensure the process is done respectfully.

Ethical issues generally arise in cases involving life support, and they have served to greatly muddle opportunities for organ transplant. If doctors, hospital administrators, lawyers, and bioethicists can resolve these issues, many more organs would likely become available. The 100,000 or so patients on organ donor waiting lists would greatly benefit. —

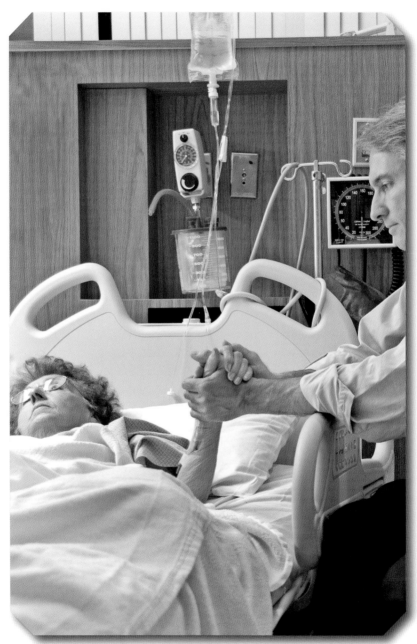

Making the decision to take a loved one off life support can be difficult.

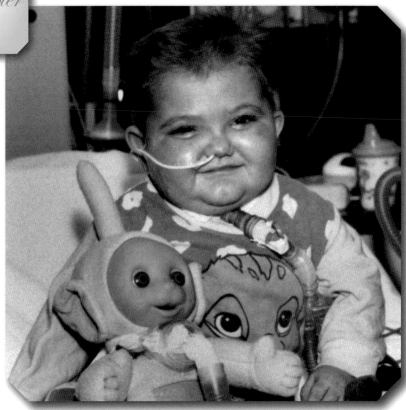

Two-year-old Brendon Ednie received a heart, two lungs, and a liver in 1998.

ORGANS FOR TRANSPLANT

*M*ost people are not likely to give a lot of thought to their pancreases. If the pancreas does its job efficiently, the person will not be aware of it. The pancreas enables the body to digest food and produces vital chemicals such as insulin, which helps turn sugar into energy. When the pancreas fails to produce insulin, a person develops diabetes. Many diabetics are able to live long lives by receiving daily injections of insulin, maintaining a healthy diet, exercising, or taking medicine. Many, however, also face severe consequences that could include blindness, loss of fingers and toes, kidney failure, heart disease, and stroke. Diabetes can be fatal, and there is no known cure.

In the 1960s, surgeons began to experiment with pancreas transplants in dogs. In 1966, the first human received a pancreas transplant but lived only two months. Subsequent surgeries produced results that were not much better. In the 1990s, doctors solved most of the problems pertaining to pancreas transplants, which mainly regarded how to keep the organ from leaking. Surgeons developed a method of draining

Advocate for Donation

Former Dallas Cowboys football player Ron Springs suffered from diabetes, which led to kidney failure. After waiting for a donor kidney for three years, Springs received an organ from Everson Walls, his friend and former teammate. The operation in early 2007 was regarded as a success. However, seven months later, Springs lapsed into a coma after undergoing an unrelated surgery. As of 2010, he remained in the coma and doctors did not expect him to recover.

Nevertheless, Walls does not regret donating his kidney to his friend. Walls continues to maintain an active life and has become an advocate for organ donation. "It was tough for me to accept being labeled a hero," Walls said. "What I did for Ron was unconditional. I wasn't looking for anything."[1]

the organ into the patient's bowel. As of 2010, pancreas transplants were still relatively rare because there are serious side effects, and finding acceptable donor matches is difficult. Often, a pancreas transplant is performed with a kidney transplant to ensure that the patient's kidney is healthy enough to resist damage related to the diabetes. Approximately 300 to 400 pancreas-only transplants are performed each year.

The fact that surgeons were able to solve the unique problems

Donating Brains to Science

After former pro football player Andre Waters died by suicide, his survivors agreed to donate his brain to a study exploring the connection between contact sports and traumatic brain injuries. During his career, Waters, a hard-hitting defensive player, suffered a number of concussions. An autopsy on Waters's brain revealed that the organ had severely deteriorated. Doctors said his brain resembled that of an 85-year-old Alzheimer's disease patient. Alzheimer's is a debilitating illness that causes mostly older people to lose their memories and other cognitive abilities. At the time of his death, Waters was 44 years old.

Since 2008, more than a dozen athletes have agreed to donate their brains to science following their deaths. The project, known as the Sports Legacy Institute, is headed by Chris Nowinski. A Harvard University graduate and former pro wrestler, Nowinski sustained numerous concussions during his career in the ring. Since retiring, he has suffered from many symptoms, including migraine headaches, insomnia, and mild depression.

In addition to football players and wrestlers, Nowinski has approached hockey players, boxers, and others who engage in contact sports. "A few people cut me off and said, 'So you want my brain?'" says Nowinski. "But the usual answer is, 'Sure, I'm not going to need it when I'm dead.'"[2]

associated with pancreas transplants illustrates how much transplant science has progressed since Louis Washkansky died 18 days following his heart transplant in 1967. Nevertheless, because they are major surgeries, organ transplants are still regarded as the cure of last resort for many patients.

Why the Heart Fails

Cardiovascular disease is regarded as the number-one health concern in the United States. One common cardiovascular disease is hypertension, or high blood pressure. This causes the heart to work harder to pump blood throughout the body. Heart attacks are another common occurrence. A heart attack happens when blood flow is cut off to the heart. Congestive heart failure occurs when the heart slows down and fails to pump enough blood to maintain the body and its organs. Strokes, which occur when blood vessels that supply the brain are blocked, are also common. Many factors cause cardiovascular disease, including fatty diets, substance abuse, smoking, obesity, and lack of exercise. Other causes include illnesses and infections, aging, and a family history of cardiovascular disease.

When an organ becomes available, it must be transported quickly. AirNet is an airline that often transports human organs.

In the United States, approximately 2,000 people a year receive donor hearts. Candidates for heart transplant are those who cannot be treated through any other means and who stand to benefit from the surgery. They are carefully screened by transplant centers. Rosemary Rangle, a social worker in the heart transplant unit at William Osler Hospital in Brampton, Ontario, says:

> We eliminate those with a serious medical condition that a transplant can't help, such as cancer . . . morbid obesity, AIDS, liver disease—anything life threatening. We want to save lives, but to do that, we sometimes have to say no to some patients so we can give the heart to somebody more likely to benefit. We can't waste organs.[3]

KIDNEYS

Far more patients—approximately 16,000—receive donor kidneys in the United States each year. Approximately 6,000 of the donated kidneys come from live donors who can survive with a single kidney. In most cases, live donors are family members or close friends of the patients.

Typically, people who need kidney transplants suffer from end-stage

The Need for Human Skin

Human skin is sought by institutions that require samples for experimentation, particularly as part of cancer research. Human skin also is needed to train firefighters, paramedics, and doctors in treating burn victims. Because skin samples come from every area of the body, tissue banks seek the donation of entire corpses.

"There is a major shortage of human tissue in this country," said Donna Goyette, director of community relations for Science Care, a bank that acquires skin and other tissue samples for research and training purposes. "If we want to advance medicine, and if we want cures for cancer and neurological disorders, we can't do that using plastic or synthetic materials."[4]

renal disease (ESRD). The two most common causes
of ESRD are diabetes and high blood pressure.
Diabetes breaks down the ability of the kidneys to
filter blood, causing important proteins to be lost
in the urine. High blood pressure can damage small
blood vessels, which are prevalent in kidneys.

The Liver

The most common disease that leads to liver
failure is hepatitis, which is spread by a virus in
an infected person's blood. It often afflicts drug
abusers who share needles and people who engage
in unprotected sex. Blood transfusions also spread
hepatitis before 1991, when protective measures were
put in place.

Hepatitis causes cirrhosis, or scarring of the
liver. When the liver becomes thick with scar tissue,
blood flow in the organ is reduced. As the liver
becomes starved for blood, it fails to do its job of
manufacturing proteins for the body. A major
cause of cirrhosis is hepatitis C. Approximately
4 million people in the United States currently
have hepatitis C, and the illness kills as many as
10,000 patients a year. Annually, only an estimated
6,300 patients receive liver transplants.

THE LUNGS

Emphysema is a disease of the lungs. The walls of the lungs lose their elasticity, trapping air inside the lung's air sacs. Another lung disease is alpha-1-antitrypsin-deficiency, in which a person lacks a protein that protects the lung against deterioration. Cystic fibrosis is an inherited disease that causes a buildup of mucus in the lungs that blocks airflow.

Lung transplants are regarded as particularly complicated. For years, doctors struggled with leakage, bleeding, and infection. Harvard Medical School transplant surgeon Nicholas L. Tilney explains that a lung "is always open to the outside environment [because of the airway that leads to it] and more at risk from external hazards than truly internal organs."[5] By the 1980s, many of the complications associated with lung transplants had been solved. But compared to other organ transplants, lung transplants are still relatively rare. Approximately 1,500 lung transplants are performed each year.

Transplanting the Cornea

The cornea is a layer of clear tissue that covers the pupil. Shaped like a dome, the cornea bends light as it strikes the eye, directing it onto a lens just behind the pupil. If the cornea becomes damaged, either through an accident or disease, it can be removed and replaced with a cornea supplied by a donor. According to the Eye Bank Association of America, some 40,000 cornea transplants are conducted each year.

A Rare Surgery

Transplants of small intestines are even rarer. In the United States, fewer than 200 people receive donor small intestines each year. Many of the patients are infants born with defective intestines. Adults who suffer from a damaging cell condition known as necrosis are also candidates for the procedure. Still, it is seldom performed, at least in adults. Surgeons can often repair the small intestine without replacing the entire organ, which is nearly 23 feet (7 m) long in most adults.

Before doctors perform an intestinal transplant, they usually recommend the patient undergo total parenteral nutrition to see if this method is a better option than surgery. In this process, nutrition is delivered to the blood through an intravenous (IV) tube, bypassing the diseased or damaged digestive system.

However, some patients develop infections or other complications from receiving their food through IV tubes. They have no choice other than to submit to the extremely radical transplant surgery.

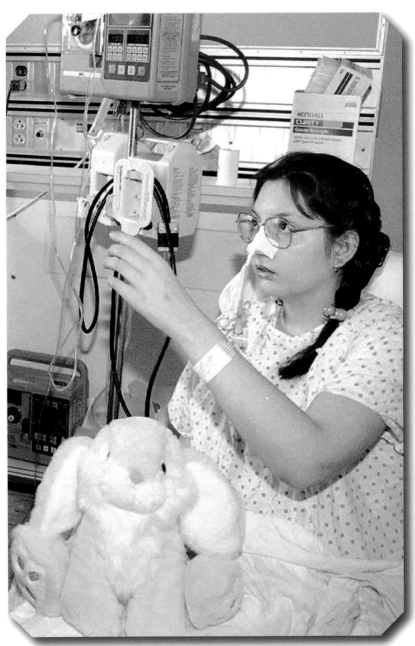

Rondie Ann Harris recovered in the hospital after receiving
a new large and small intestine in 1996.

Michael Miraglia, right, talks with transplant surgeon Norman Shumway.

ORGAN RECIPIENTS

oon after Michael Miraglia was told he
would need a heart transplant, the Castro
Valley, California, man was hospitalized at Stanford
University Hospital to await a donor heart. There, he
was housed in a room with another patient waiting

for a heart transplant. This man, whom Miraglia knew only as John, was an inmate from a local prison.

When a donor heart was found, doctors made the decision to provide the heart to John. The inmate underwent surgery and was eventually returned to prison to complete his sentence. However, the doctors' decision leaked out and made the local news. The situation sparked hostile reactions. People questioned how doctors could deny a life-saving measure to a law-abiding citizen and choose instead to provide it to a prison inmate. "You have to wonder if a law-abiding, tax-paying citizen drew one last breath while Jailhouse Joe was getting a second wind," wrote Steve Lopez, a columnist for the *Los Angeles Times*.[1]

For his part, Miraglia understood the doctors' decision was based on John's need, the likelihood of organ acceptance, and his own physical

Adopting John the Inmate

When Michael Miraglia and the inmate known as John shared a hospital room as they waited for new hearts, the Miraglia family learned that John was under security watch. This meant he was unable to receive visits from friends or family members or even telephone calls. So the Miraglias "adopted" John. They asked their friends and family members to pray as much for John as they did for Michael. "It is so hard to imagine anyone going through this ordeal without loved ones and friends to support them," Michael's wife, Cheryl, told friends.[2]

condition. The physicians believed Miraglia's body was too weak at the time to undergo the difficult surgery. But even those circumstances did not matter to Miraglia. He understood that all transplant patients are equal, and decisions about who gets organs are based on medical factors, not a person's perceived worth to society.

Confined to his hospital room, Miraglia watched the growing criticism of the Stanford doctors. He found himself thinking, "What? Are they kidding? How could choosing to save a person's life be unethical?"[3] Eventually, Miraglia did grow strong enough and received a new heart. After his release from the hospital, he remained in touch with John and visited him in prison. Miraglia says he feels a close bond to the man who received the heart that could very well have been implanted in his own chest.

WHO DECIDES?

As the case involving Miraglia and John illustrates, decisions about who gets donated organs are not based on the patients' résumés, their status in society, or the amount in their bank accounts. Rather, patients selected to receive new organs are those who have been judged by their doctors to be most in need and most likely to survive the procedure. However, the backlash against the doctors for giving the heart to the inmate demonstrates the controversy surrounding the issue of who "deserves" an organ. Many also wonder who should be in charge of prioritizing the possible recipients.

In the United States, the Organ Procurement and Transplantation Network manages donor organs. Established by Congress in 1984, the group is administered by Virginia-

The Need for Two Organs

In 1993, Pennsylvania Governor Robert P. Casey received a new heart and liver. Suffering from amyloidosis, his body's immune system had attacked his vital organs. He kept his illness secret until his condition turned critical. On June 12, he was placed on the waiting list for a new heart and liver. Within 24 hours, he received both donor organs. At the time, the average waiting period for a new heart was 198 days, while liver transplant patients waited an average of 67 days.

After Casey's surgery, it was revealed that six patients had priority over Casey for new hearts, and two patients had higher priority for new livers. This added fuel to the charge that the governor had been given preferential treatment.

But Casey's case was unique because he needed two organs at once. His condition would continue to be critical if he received only one organ and remained on the waiting list for the other. "In this case, the real issue is whether those needing two organs should be taken ahead of those needing only one," says Robert M. Veatch, professor of medical ethics at Georgetown University in Washington DC. "There is a good case for such a priority because it could be a long time before two suitable organs again become available simultaneously."[4]

based United Network for Organ Sharing, a nonprofit group that has contracted with the federal government.

The network maintains a computer database linking hospitals, physicians, foundations, and other medical institutions. When an organ becomes available, the computer matches it with a needy patient. Nationally, patients are ranked according to their need, with those in the most critical conditions given higher rankings. Certain medical factors are also considered. For example, the blood type of the donor and recipient must match, as should body types. For example, an adult cannot be a candidate for an organ from an infant.

Geography is also a factor. Patients are given higher consideration for organs that become available close to home. If the need arises, an organ can be refrigerated and flown cross-country to an awaiting transplant patient. As conditions change, patients can also be moved up the list.

Organ Costs

Transplants are among the most expensive medical procedures, with most costing hundreds of thousands of dollars. In the case of the inmate John,

Average Costs of Organ Transplants*

Organ	Heart	Lung	Liver
Procurement	$89,900	$40,871	$59,100
Hospital	$383,300	$209,329	$248,100
Physician	$40,300	$33,200	$66,900
Evaluation	$22,900	$20,000	$25,900
Follow-up Care	$93,000	$65,600	$88,500
Drugs	$29,400	$30,500	$31,100
Total	$658,800	$399,500	$519,600

Organ	Kidney	Pancreas	Intestine
Procurement	$58,300	$66,200	$75,449
Hospital	$74,500	$107,100	$602,451
Physician	$21,500	$24,600	$87,100
Evaluation	$14,600	$14,700	$41,700
Follow-up Care	$48,000	$48,300	$78,500
Drugs	$29,500	$36,400	$23,400
Total	$246,400	$297,300	$908,600

*Costs are for the first year following the transplant. Statistics are based on 2007 prices.

Source: TransplantLiving.org, <www.transplantliving.org/beforethetransplant/finance/costs.aspx>.

Organ transplants are costly surgical procedures.

the taxpayers of California had to pay the bill, which came to more than $900,000. Some people object to this cost. Others believe that saving a life is always

Medicare and Medicaid

Medicare and Medicaid are government-run health insurance programs. Medicare is geared toward people over the age of 65, while Medicaid offers health benefits to low-income people.

The concept of government-sponsored health care was proposed by President Harry Truman in 1945. President Lyndon Johnson signed bills authorizing Medicare and Medicaid in 1965.

While these programs have become cherished institutions, they are also highly controversial because they are so expensive. Some estimates had shown that, in 2009, Medicare would cost the federal government approximately $480 billion, which was approximately 13 percent of that year's federal budget. These programs are so expensive, in part, because they offer health coverage to those most likely to need medical treatment as opposed to healthier, working-age people.

worth the cost, no matter who the patient is.

Poor people, as well as the elderly, are covered under federal medical assistance programs such as Medicaid and Medicare. Nevertheless, many people find themselves facing financial hardships when they undergo organ transplants.

Many people are covered by private health insurance, but insurance does not pay all the bills. Typically, insurance companies cover about 80 percent of the cost of transplants. Other patients have no insurance or have limited policies that do not cover a majority of their expenses. These people often have to rely on charities and similar organizations to raise money for their transplants. Friends and neighbors have staged fundraisers for transplant patients. For many families, this financial hardship adds to the stress of waiting for an organ.

MICKEY MANTLE'S STORY

Occasionally, and particularly in the case of a celebrity, charges surface suggesting the patient was unfairly moved to the head of the line. That happened in 1995 when baseball legend Mickey Mantle received a new liver just one day after his name was entered into the national database. At the time, more than 4,600 others were waiting for liver transplants. Mantle's liver had deteriorated due to hepatitis and cirrhosis.

A resident of Dallas, Texas, Mantle received a new liver through the Dallas-based Southwest Organ Bank. Within days of Mantle's surgery, the bank was flooded with phone calls from liver patients in the area demanding to know why Mantle was moved ahead of them. Other organ banks across the country received similar calls. Many people wondered if Mantle had been given special treatment because of his fame. Organ bank workers had to assure the callers that had not been the case.

Back in Texas, doctors insisted that Mantle deserved a new liver because he faced certain death without it. Goran Klintmalm, a transplant physician at Baylor University Medical Center, where the former baseball great received his new liver,

Mantle Donor Cards

Mickey Mantle's liver transplant may have raised questions about how donation priorities are set, but there is no question that it helped the cause of organ donation. Following Mantle's death, the former player's charity, the Mickey Mantle Foundation, distributed thousands of organ donor cards featuring Mantle's image to fans at baseball stadiums. "My father made this a personal issue," said Mantle's son, Danny. "We want to keep his commitment and dream alive. There are thousands of people waiting for organs."[7]

defended Mantle's high priority for the transplant. He said, "There is no way you can circumvent the system."[5]

Mickey Mantle's situation raised another issue regarding the ethics of organ transplantation. Mantle's liver damage was self-inflicted. He had been a heavy drinker his entire adult life, which had caused the cirrhosis. That fact made some wonder if people responsible for their own conditions should be given lower priority than patients who are the victims of disease. Arthur Caplan, a University of Pennsylvania bioethicist, said, "Spending $300,000 for a liver transplant for somebody who brought harm upon himself is not a prudent use of scarce money and scarce livers."[6] Even among those who wholly support organ donation, deciding who receives priority for a new organ is a muddled issue.

Independent physicians who looked into the case later concluded that the physicians acted correctly in moving Mantle to the top of the list. He died of cancer at the age of 63, approximately two months after receiving his new liver.

STEVE JOBS'S LIVER CONTROVERSY

Mickey Mantle is not the only celebrity whose organ transplant has spurred discussion about the equity of organ donation methods. In 2004, Steve Jobs, cofounder and CEO of Apple Inc., announced that he suffered from a rare form of pancreatic cancer. The cancer had produced a tumor, which was removed quickly and successfully. However, in early 2009, Jobs was noticeably thinner, and rumors emerged about his health. He announced in January that he would take a leave from the company to address his health issues. Doctors had been concerned that the cancer in his pancreas would spread to other organs and recommended he receive a liver transplant. In early 2009, Jobs underwent surgery to receive a new liver.

Receiving a liver transplant is fairly routine. But what drew the public's attention to his case was that Jobs, a California resident, received his new liver in Tennessee. The average wait time for a liver in Tennessee is 48 days, compared to a national median wait time of 306 days. Jobs did not directly pay for his liver, and he did not pay to get ahead of another person on the list. When a liver became available in Tennessee, Jobs was deemed the most needy recipient of the liver. But Jobs was able to pay for the costs of being flown to Tennessee immediately. Because he could afford the expenses of quick transportation, Jobs could register in a place with a lower wait time and, therefore, have a better chance of receiving a liver. Many are questioning the ethics of the circumstance, claiming that cases such as these give the wealthy an unfair advantage over those who cannot afford such measures.

Apple CEO Steve Jobs underwent a liver transplant in 2009.

Some people keep donor cards with them in their purses or wallets.

ORGAN DONORS

A 2005 poll commissioned by the U.S. Health Resources and Services Administration found that an overwhelming majority of people in the United States—93 percent—support organ donation. At the same time, it reported that just more than half of these people have made arrangements via donor cards or driver's licenses to donate their organs. And just a fraction of those, approximately 8,000, will provide organs each year.

What causes the gap between those who support organ donation and those who have designated themselves as donors? Part of the reason may be that the poll itself is flawed—many experts do not believe it accurately reflects the attitudes of people in the United States. Organ donation seems like a noble and courageous cause. Many may feel awkward telling the pollster they would not be donors.

"We know that when we do surveys like this, more people claim to have done the right thing than do the right thing," says pollster Humphrey Taylor, who has conducted surveys on organ donation. He also questions the poll's numbers about designated donors: "I think if half of all U.S. adults really had registered [as organ donors], we would be in much better shape than we are, so I am skeptical of those numbers."[1]

A reason for the shortage of donors is apathy. Planning the use of one's organs after death is not a top priority for most people. Also, some experts blame the shortage of organ donors on the failure of the U.S. health care system. Many believe that if donors received compensation for their organs,

more would be available, which would make more organ transplant surgeries possible.

On the other hand, a devotion to highway safety has meant fewer deaths in accidents. Decades ago, wearing seatbelts in cars was optional. Today, all states mandate their use. Most cars today are equipped with airbags, and legislators and police have cracked down on drunk driving.

The Pool of Donors

A slang term for motorcycles is "donor-cycles." The name came about because of the perceived danger of motorcycle riding. Some people have wondered if there is a relationship between riders who do not wear helmets—who are also organ donors—and organ donation rates.

The International Transport Forum in Paris, France, compiled statistics on annual fatalities of motor vehicle drivers and their passengers in the United States. According to their report, motorcycle rider fatalities rose from 2,116 in 1997 to 3,661 in 2003—an increase of 73 percent.

The rise is due to a trend among states to relax laws that make helmet wearing on motorcycles mandatory. Some states have relaxed their laws under pressure from motorcycle enthusiasts, who insist that wearing a helmet should be a matter of personal choice. Some states have no helmet laws at all. In 2003, Pennsylvania lawmakers repealed the state's mandatory helmet law. According to a University of Pittsburgh report made five years after the repeal, the number of head-injury deaths among motorcyclists rose 66 percent. Some reports suggest that repealing helmet requirement laws may actually increase the number of organ donors, although the increase is very small.

Meanwhile, brain surgery techniques have improved, so more people survive traumatic brain injuries. Although the number of people who donate organs has steadily increased in recent years, it could be argued that the pool of prime donors—healthy people who die in tragic accidents—has grown smaller.

RELIGIOUS OPPOSITION

Many people harbor qualms about organ donation because of their religious backgrounds. Some religions specifically oppose the surgical techniques necessary to transplant organs.

For example, many of the 1.1 million Jehovah's Witnesses in the United States refuse to accept blood transfusions. They interpret certain biblical references to mean they cannot share the blood of others, which precludes them as potential organ donors and recipients.

Bloodless Transplants

In 1999, physicians in Belgium performed a liver transplant on a member of the Jehovah's Witnesses. They found a way to do the procedure without relying on a blood transfusion, which is against the religion's beliefs. The chemical erythropoietin was injected into the patient's body before surgery. Erythropoietin enhances the production of white blood cells, which enables the patient to sustain the loss of blood common during surgery.

Paul Gillies, a spokesman for the church, said the religion's leaders are optimistic that such procedures can become routine. This would enable Jehovah's Witnesses to participate in organ transplants. "We approach this subject from the Bible's perspective, and the medical profession [is] looking for alternatives," Gillies said. "It seems that we are coming together, even though we have been walking down two different roads."[2]

Curing the Disabled Organ

The founder of the Christian Science movement, Mary Baker Eddy, believed that people could cure themselves of illness. She stressed an element of spiritual healing, not medical treatment, that could be attained if the patient found a way to rise above sin. Although members of the Christian Science religion sometimes do opt to receive an organ transplant, many lean on spiritual healing instead.

Some Christian Science followers also adhere to principles that preclude them from receiving or donating organs. Many refuse to participate in medical procedures, particularly those that require drugs, which are a necessary part of the transplant process.

In Japan, the Shinto tradition respects the wholeness and purity of the body even after death. Members of the Shinto faith believe that removing an organ is a form of desecration of a corpse. They do not permit organs to be harvested from their loved ones, nor do they accept organs. As such, organ transplants are rare in Japan.

Acts of Charity

Many religious groups do support organ donation. Like members of the Shinto faith, Muslims believe that the body should remain whole after death. However, supporting charity is a main principle of their faith. Because of this, Muslims support organ donation.

Jewish people believe that life is of high value, so the faith is generally in support of organ donation to save a life. However, Orthodox Jews regard life to be over when the heart stops beating, not when the brain dies. Therefore, many Orthodox Jews do not authorize doctors to turn off the heart and lung machines of loved ones who are brain-dead.

Christians generally support organ donation as an act of charity. Typically, though, religious leaders believe organ donation is a decision that must be made by individuals and their families. Therefore, many people find themselves conflicted. In particular, fundamentalist Christians question whether close relatives have the right to shut off a machine that is keeping a loved one's heart beating. "While the Bible does not speak against organ donation, people who revere God's word still feel a certain amount of reservation concerning the harvesting of organs— and for good reason," says Brad

Organ Donation Endorsed by John Paul II

In 2000, Pope John Paul II urged Catholics to donate their organs. He said, "It is surely a reason for satisfaction that many sick people, who until recently could only expect death or at best a painful and restricted existence, can now recover more or less fully through replacement of a diseased organ with a healthy donated one. We should rejoice that medicine, in its service of life, has found in organ transplantation a new way of serving this human family, precisely by safeguarding that fundamental good of the person."[3]

Harrub, a Nashville, Tennessee, neuroscientist and fundamentalist Christian educator. He adds,

> There is nothing ethically wrong in recovering organs from the dead, but most successful organ transplants require that any prospective organs be kept alive with blood and oxygen flowing through them until they are removed from the body. This quandary is indeed problematic, for we cannot, and must not, support the termination of life in favor of organ donation. [4]

Harrub and other fundamentalist Christians worry that standards have been modified. Relatives are turning off machines at earlier stages, blurring the line between life and death. He points to a decision made by the American Medical Association (AMA). The AMA endorses the commencement of organ harvesting from anencephalic infants—babies born missing much of their brains and skulls—before their actual deaths. He says,

> How many more laws and definitions will be changed in the future as the demand for usable organs continues to outnumber the supply[?] . . . We must carefully determine, in light of the teachings found within God's word, whether a respirator is simply oxygenating a corpse or sustaining a living human being. [5]

Deacon Richard H. Adams urged those in his New Jersey congregation to sign up as organ donors.

Some wealthy people travel to impoverished places, such as these Indian slums, to pay a person to donate his or her kidney.

Transplant Tourism

Although some patients receive transplants quickly, others must wait a long time for suitable donors and may become desperate. This desperation can lead them to take extreme actions.

The Kidney Trade

In recent years, kidney disease patients in the United States have been willing to travel to India and other nations to take part in a thriving, but illegal, organ industry. Because the body can function on a single kidney, many poor people are willing to have one of their kidneys extracted for a price. The kidneys are then sold.

As of 2010, more than 80,000 people remained on the waiting list for kidneys in the United States, and they could stay on the list for several years. In India, however, a desperate patient who can afford the price—$25,000 or more—can obtain a kidney quickly. The donor sees little of that money, usually just $1,000 to $2,500. The remainder goes to the kidney traffickers and the doctors willing to perform the surgeries. Many of these traffickers are able to make large amounts of money and sometimes become quite wealthy.

The surgeries are often performed in unhygienic conditions. Germs can

The "Kidney Bazaar"

Poverty is so overwhelming in parts of Pakistan that the country's press has dubbed the nation a "kidney bazaar" because of the Pakistanis' willingness to sell their organs.

In Sultanpur Mor, a village in eastern Pakistan, Nassem Kausar has sold one of her kidneys. So have her sister, six brothers, five sisters-in-law, and two nephews. Each received about $2,500 for his or her organ. "We do this because of our poverty," Kausar told a reporter.[1]

**Approximate Kidney Prices
on the International Black Market**

Country	Price
China	$65,000
Colombia	$80,000
Iraq	$20,000
Pakistan	$15,000–$40,000
Philippines	$35,000–$85,000
Russia	$25,000
South Africa	$120,000
Turkey	$145,000

Source: Michelle Tsai. "Organs for Sale: Where in the World Can I Buy a Heart?" *Wired*.
20 April 2007. <www.wired.com/wired/archive/15.04/start_page7.html>.

The price of an illegally obtained kidney can vary greatly.

lead to infections, which complicate the healing process. One typical story is that of taxi driver Guna Ponraj. In Chennai, India, Ponraj was promised $2,500 for one of his kidneys. He consented and was ultimately paid just half of the promised fee. He has suffered complications from his surgery. The constant pain has often forced him to miss work. Ponraj regrets his decision and feels he was misled.

"I can sell my kidney and become rich, I thought," he has said.[2]

An International Business

Many wealthy Saudis and Jordanians in need of kidneys have found donors in the slums of Cairo, Egypt. Illegal commerce in organs has also been uncovered in Albania and Colombia. Because of the scarcity of organs in Japan due to the principles of the Shinto faith, some wealthy Japanese patients have hired gangsters to search for organs outside Japan. In one case, police uncovered a group of Japanese organ traffickers looking for organs in Boston that they intended to send back to clients in Japan.

Some organ traffickers have established offices in the United States. For hefty fees, they will locate donor organs in other countries. They take care of all the arrangements. The U.S. patient flies to the donor's country, where

The Istanbul Declaration

In 2008, medical officials from 78 countries met in Istanbul, Turkey. They drafted a statement condemning the international black market trade in organs. The Istanbul Declaration urges world governments to outlaw organ trafficking. The declaration states, "Organ trafficking and transplant tourism violate the principles of equity, justice and respect for human dignity and should be prohibited." The document also states that "transplant commercialism targets impoverished and otherwise vulnerable donors, [which] leads inexorably to inequity and injustice."[3]

The 2004 Indian Ocean Tsunami

On December 26, 2004, an enormous tsunami hit Southeast Asia, South Asia, and East Africa. Tsunamis are caused by earthquakes, and geology experts estimated the earthquake that caused the 2004 tsunami was the strongest earthquake on Earth since 1964. Some of the tsunami's largest waves traveled as much as 500 miles per hour (800 km/hr) and were 50 feet (15 meters) high. Virtually no one was prepared for the tsunami, and approximately 228,000 people were killed. Millions more were displaced.

In the aftermath, aid organizations set up refugee camps for homeless victims. However, these camps became a prime target for organ brokers to prey upon poor people who had no means of income. One newspaper reported that as many as 150 tsunami survivors, most of them women, sold their organs to make money.

the operation is performed. One U.S. organ broker named Mitch (he refused to give his last name to a reporter) boasted that he has charged as much as $85,000 to find a kidney for a desperate patient.

Buying and selling organs is illegal in most countries, including India. To someone facing death from kidney failure, however, breaking the law is often of little concern. In addition, the laws are rarely enforced. In India, for example, a 1994 law prohibited anyone other than a close relative from participating in a live donation of a kidney. Still, brokers who black-market organs in India seem to have little trouble finding ways around the law.

PREYING ON TSUNAMI VICTIMS

Some kidney traffickers have targeted the refugee camps that were established following the 2004 Indian Ocean tsunami. Years after

The 2004 Indian Ocean tsunami left millions homeless. Many did not have the means to provide for their families and fell victim to organ trafficking.

the tsunami, tens of thousands of people remain homeless in several Asian countries. Some refugees willingly sell their kidneys to earn money to buy food for their families. In many cases, however, traffickers cheat the donors out of their fees by disappearing following the surgeries.

In 2007, after a police crackdown in several Indian refugee camps nearly wiped out the illegal organ trade, riots broke out. Refugees complained that police had denied them one of their few ways of providing for their families.

Organs from Prisoners

More than kidneys are available on the black market. In China, the government has uncovered a network of rogue physicians who traffic in organs harvested from prisoners who have been executed. The practice likely takes place in Taiwan and Singapore, too, and it continues despite efforts by authorities to stop it.

Harry Wu, a Chinese human rights activist, says,

I interviewed a doctor who routinely participated in removing kidneys from condemned prisoners. In one case she said, breaking

---

Executions in China

The number of inmates executed in China is a closely guarded state secret. According to human rights group Amnesty International, the number could be as high as 8,000 executions a year. In contrast, approximately 60 prison inmates undergo the death sentence each year in the United States.

Human rights activists charge that government officials in China are anxious to execute inmates because of the widespread black market for organs. This trade benefits doctors, prison administrators, and others. The Chinese government has claimed to have cracked down on the market. In 2006, the government issued new regulations specifically banning the sale of organs harvested from executed prisoners, but human rights activists are not convinced that the trade has been wiped out. "Given the high commercial value of organs, it is doubtful the new regulations will have an effect," says Mark Allison, an Amnesty International official.[4]

Medical officials in other countries have taken steps they hope will reduce the Chinese organ black market. In Australia, for example, two major transplant centers, Princess Alexandra Hospital and Prince Charles Hospital, have banned the admission of Chinese doctors for transplant training.

down in the telling, that she had even participated in a surgery in which two kidneys were removed from a living, anaesthetized prisoner late at night. The following morning the prisoner was executed by a bullet to the head.[5]

LEGAL IN SOME COUNTRIES

Some countries, including the Philippines and Iran, allow donors to legally sell their organs. The governments do so, in part, to help regulate the trade and limit abusive practices. Still, critics charge that legalizing the trade has not been successful. The system is corrupted by government officials who accept bribes from unscrupulous traffickers, they say. For example, Nancy Scheper-Hughes contends that Iranian officials appointed to oversee the trade have turned into black-market brokers themselves. She has established a watchdog group, Organs Watch, to report abuses in organ donation.

Forced Transplants in Egypt

Some poor people seeking work in Egypt claim they have been forced to "donate" their kidneys. Three Egyptians—Abdel Hamid, Ahmed Ibrahim, and Ashraf Zakaria—told reporters that they answered advertisements seeking work. They were told they would have to undergo medical examinations. During their exams, the doctors told them that they suffered from kidney infections and would have to undergo immediate surgeries. When they woke up in the hospital, each was missing a kidney. As for the man who promised them jobs, he had disappeared.

Also, donors who are paid legally do not necessarily receive more money than illegal donors. Mitch, the U.S. organ broker, pointed out that many kidneys are available in the Philippines, which keeps prices low. He says, "The donors are in such huge supply where it's legal, like the Philippines, so they have to accept [an] average of $3,000."[6]

Proponents of regulating organ donation feel the advantages outweigh the ethical issues. The practice does help decrease the amount of stolen organs, for example. Also, they believe it will make more life-saving organs available. ⁓

*These Filipino men show their scars from surgery.
They sold their kidneys to earn money.*

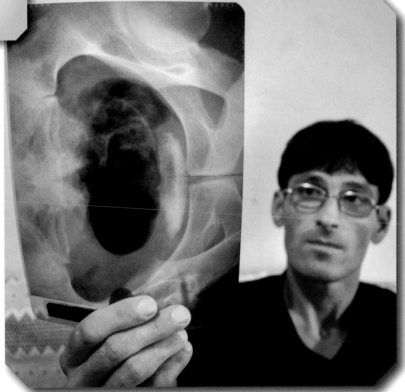

Safet Music holds up an X-ray of a kidney he is willing to sell. He is desperate to earn money.

COMPENSATION
FOR DONORS

As the term states, people are organ donors—they are expected to *donate* their organs. If they are deceased, their survivors can expect to receive no compensation for providing the organs to others. In 1984, Congress adopted the National Organ Transplant Act that outlawed a commercial trade in organs. But given the shortage of donors in the United States, as well as the illegal trade in many countries, many physicians and bioethicists have suggested rethinking the ban on organ sales.

DEFRAYING COSTS

Even those opposed to selling organs may believe donors should receive some payment to cover costs associated with surgeries. In 2004, President George W. Bush signed the Organ Donation and Recovery Improvement Act. It provides financial assistance to live organ donors to reimburse them for their costs. In many cases, donors undergo lengthy recoveries. The federal law helps ease the stress of remaining out of work during this time.

Approximately a dozen states have enacted tax breaks for live donors. In Wisconsin, the first state to pass such a law, donors can receive tax breaks

Black Market in Cadavers

Michael Mastromarino, a former dentist, was convicted in 2008 in a scheme to pay funeral directors for access to cadavers. Mastromarino harvested body parts from the cadavers. For the most part, he sold the body parts to biotechnology firms for research purposes. Some of the skin was grafted onto burn victims and others in need of skin transplants.

Mastromarino and his conspirators are alleged to have illegally harvested parts from approximately 1,000 bodies. Among that number was the body of Alistair Cooke, the long-time host of *Masterpiece Theater* on PBS. He died in 2004 at the age of 95. Mastromarino was sentenced to at least 18 years in prison.

of up to $10,000. On the federal level, an income tax reduction for donors of up to $5,000 went into consideration by Congress in 2009.

Many experts do not believe the reimbursements or tax incentives go far enough. They say more people would designate themselves as organ donors if they could be assured their survivors would receive monetary compensation. Such programs could go a long way toward reducing patient waiting lists, they argue.

Some people point out that people are already paid for providing various other parts of their bodies, such as plasma, hair to wig makers, and sperm and eggs to fertilization clinics. ". . . [O]nly organs are excluded from markets," argues University of Chicago law professor Michele Goodwin. "It's time to end this rule, and save lives."[1]

Hastening Death

University of Virginia bio-ethics professor James Childress worries that family members may pre-maturely pull their dying relatives off life support if they know they can sell the organs. "Many people don't sign donor cards now because of distrust or mistrust," he says. "They worry about being declared dead pre-maturely, or even having their deaths hastened, if they have signed a donor card. Well, they would certainly be reluctant to enter a futures market, to sign a futures contract, when the only barrier to the delivery of their organs is the fact that they're not dead yet."[2]

U.S. BLACK MARKET

Proponents for legalizing organ sales point out that an illegal commerce in kidneys already exists in the United States, as it does in other countries. A number of respected programs in the United States were found to have transplanted illegal organs in U.S. hospitals. Although the practice is rare in the United States, it does happen.

Web sites matching recipients with donors are common. Many wealthy people are reluctant to travel to third-world nations to undergo surgery by unknown physicians. Instead, they pay to fly donors to the United States so that surgery is performed close to home. In some cases, willing donors have been found in the United States.

According to organ trade watchdog Nancy Scheper-Hughes, the total cost to the kidney recipient of finding a donor and arranging transportation and lodging in the United States can be $150,000 or more. Scheper-Hughes stated,

> People all over were telling me that they didn't have to go to a third world hospital, but could get the surgery done in New York, Philadelphia, or Los Angeles—at top hospitals, with top surgeons.[3]

Scheper-Hughes has brought her concerns about black market kidney transplants to several hospital administrators in the United States. They admitted they do not perform background checks on donor patients, assuming instead that the donors are close relatives or friends of the recipients. The hospitals have no system in place for detecting illegal organ sales. Scheper-Hughes says the hospital administrators promised to tighten their regulations and investigate the backgrounds of the donors.

What Is Presumed Consent?

To help fill the need for organs, many European countries have adopted a standard known as "presumed consent." Under this policy, everyone who dies is automatically regarded as an organ donor unless the individual or his or her family members have registered prior objections.

Legislation to create a presumed consent law in Great Britain was introduced in the House of Commons in 2009. Jeremy Browne, the legislator who introduced the bill, said,

> Approximately 1,000 people in the United Kingdom die every year waiting for an organ transplant because a suitable organ does not come up in time to save them. The terms of the bill therefore represent a pressing issue for those people and their families and friends.[4]

House of Commons member Stephen O'Brien opposed the bill, saying it would intrude on the rights of grieving family members. They may be startled to learn that their loved one has been taken from his or her death bed to have organs and other body parts harvested. He said, "We cannot escape the fact that this subject touches on people's notions of what is appropriate in death and on the sanctity and ownership of our bodies."[5]

Still, Scheper-Hughes suspects illegal organ trafficking in the United States is widespread. One Israeli man, Nick Rosen, told Scheper-Hughes that he was desperate for money when he saw an advertisement in a Tel Aviv newspaper seeking kidney donors. Rosen said he contacted the organ broker and was soon flown to the United States. The surgery was performed at a New York hospital. Rosen says he was paid $15,000 to sell his kidney on the black market.

Rosen says the New York doctors asked few questions. "The doctors . . . were not very curious about me," Rosen says. "We told them I was a close friend of the guy who I sold my kidney to, and that I was donating altruistically, and that was pretty much the end of it."[6]

ORGAN EXCHANGE

Those who believe the organ trade should be legalized do have some concerns. Given the abuses in Iran and other countries that allow it, proponents acknowledge that

Kidneys for Sale on eBay

In 1999, an anonymous donor offered to sell a kidney on the Internet auction site eBay. The donor set an opening price of $25,000 for the organ. Bidders offered as much as $5.7 million for the kidney before eBay officials discovered the auction and shut it down. A short time later, another donor offered to sell a kidney on the site. This time, the donor set a minimum bid price of $4 million. By the time eBay officials shut down that auction, it had received no bids.

Caryn Long's husband, Steven, died in early 2008 while waiting
for a liver transplant. He had already received two kidneys.

the trade would have to be closely regulated. They
envision a system in which a government agency
would collect the fees and pay the donors.

Psychiatrist Sally Satel, a kidney-transplant
recipient and advocate for legal commerce in
organs, says,

> *Many people need more of an incentive to give. And that's*
> *why we need to be able to compensate people who are willing*
> *to give a kidney to a stranger, to save a life. We are not talking*
> *about a classic commercial free-for-all, or a free market, or*

an eBay system. We're talking about a third-party payer. For example, today you could decide to give a kidney. You'd be called a Good Samaritan donor. . . . The only difference in a model that I'm thinking about is where you go and give your organ, and your retirement account is wired $40,000, end of story.[7]

Opponents of legalizing organ sales argue that placing price tags on body parts reduces them to the status of commodities, such as gold, crude oil, or farm crops. The value of commodities rises and falls based on market conditions. They envision dark days in which organs are put up for auction to be bid on by desperate patients. If this were to happen, they fear lower-income people would be left behind. Currently, priority is given based on need and other factors, but in a free-market system, those who could not afford to pay high fees might not get a chance

Avoiding the Cost of a Funeral

A funeral can be expensive. The American Association of Retired Persons (AARP) estimates a family can spend $10,000 or more to bury a loved one. People can arrange for their survivors to avoid the expense by donating their bodies to medical research. Several nonprofit groups have been established to accept the bodies, harvest the tissue and other usable parts, cremate the remains, and return the ashes to the family—all without cost to the family. One organization, Anatomy Gifts Registry of Hanover, Maryland, accepts approximately 50 bodies a month. The parts are used mainly to train medical students or provide organs for research purposes.

to purchase a needed organ. "There are many reasons . . . for banning the sale of organs," suggest economists Stephen J. Dubner and Steven D. Levitt. For example:

> *Some people consider it immoral to [place a value on] body parts. . . . Others fear that most organ sellers would be poor while most buyers would be rich; or that someone might be pressured into selling a kidney without fully understanding the risks.*[8]

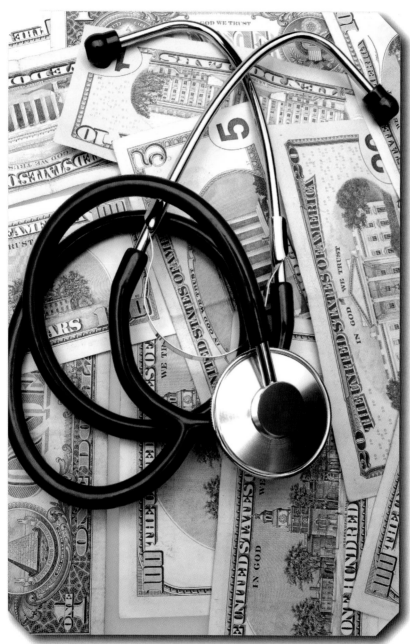

Organ transplant surgeries are expensive. Some people believe donors should receive monetary compensation for giving an organ.

Some people believe that stem cell research may make organ donation unnecessary, but the research is highly controversial.

ALTERNATIVES TO ORGAN DONATION

Years from now, people with diseased organs may not have to rely on organ donors to save their lives. If the science of stem cell therapy produces the results that its proponents expect, many debilitating diseases that cause organ failure can be wiped out. "Replacing dead pancreatic cells with young, insulin-producing . . . cells could banish diabetes, and an infusion of fresh liver cells could rejuvenate a sick liver from the inside out," says Eve Herold, public education manager for the Stem Cell Research Foundation of Clarksburg, Maryland.[1]

Stem cells are undifferentiated. This means that they have not yet formed into bone cells, blood cells, skin cells, or any other type of specialized cells. In stem cell therapy, doctors inject these undifferentiated cells into ill or debilitated patients, coaxing their bodies to replace cells damaged by diseases or accidents. "Scientists believe that these miniature powerhouses, once we understand them, will revolutionize medicine," says Herold.[2]

However, controversy has surrounded one type of stem cell

An Artificial Lung

Doctors at the University of Michigan have experimented with an artificial lung. The BioLung device is about the size of a soda can and can be implanted in a patient's chest. The patient's heart pumps blood into the device, which contains plastic fibers that draw carbon dioxide gas from the blood. This gas is exhaled, just as it would be with the help of a natural lung. As the blood passes through the device, it absorbs oxygen that has been inhaled. The blood then circulates, providing oxygen throughout the body.

therapy known as embryonic stem cell therapy. In this process, the stem cells are withdrawn from a very early form of the human embryo known as the blastocyst. When the cells are withdrawn, the embryo is destroyed. Many people in the anti-abortion movement oppose embryonic stem cell research because they believe the embryo is a human life, and destroying the embryo destroys the opportunity for it to develop into a baby. "What is the actual difference between a 1-year-old child and an embryonic child? Size and age," insists Judie Brown, president of the American Life League, which opposes embryonic stem cell research. "That is the only difference. The human being who is described as an embryo is no different than the human being who is described as a 1-year-old child."[3]

The Stem Cell Controversy

Embryonic stem cells are not drawn from a blastocyst that has embedded in a mother's womb. Rather, frozen blastocysts are obtained by researchers from in vitro fertilization clinics. These clinics aid couples who are unable to conceive children naturally. At a clinic, an egg surgically removed from a mother is fertilized with the father's sperm in a glass dish. (*In vitro* is a Latin term that means "in the glass.") After the egg is fertilized, it is returned to the womb where it develops into a fetus.

In vitro fertilization clinics typically fertilize several eggs in case the first attempt at fertilization fails. The excess blastocysts are stored in frozen nitrogen in case they are needed in the future. Eventually, most are discarded after the mother becomes pregnant. Embryonic stem cell researchers, with the consent of the parents, can obtain excess blastocysts from the clinics. Some estimated 400,000 blastocysts are frozen at in vitro fertilization clinics, and approximately 8,000 are destroyed each year in the United States.

Nevertheless, opponents of embryonic stem cell research insist that all frozen embryos should have a chance to develop into babies in the wombs of other mothers who are

An Artificial Pancreas

Many diabetics wear an insulin pump. This device delivers a steady flow of insulin to the body throughout the day. Scientists believe they are close to perfecting the pump, essentially making it an artificial pancreas. The device, which is about the size of a cell phone, includes a computer that monitors the patient's blood sugar level. When the computer determines the level is rising, it will trigger the pump to release a dose of insulin.

unable to conceive. They do not want these frozen embryos to be destroyed. In 2006, President George W. Bush held a press conference to announce his opposition to providing federal funds for embryonic stem cell research that had not already begun. During the event, Bush was accompanied by several "snowflake children." These children were born via in vitro fertilization after their embryos had spent time in a freezer. Many researchers sought private foundation funds or left the United States to continue their work in other countries where this type of research was unrestricted.

The Origins of Organ Regeneration Research

For centuries, scientists have been aware that some animals are able to regenerate damaged organs by growing new body parts on their own. Swiss naturalist Abraham Trembley made that discovery in 1740 when he experimented on a tiny animal he found swimming in a pond. Trembley named the animal "hydra" because its habits mimicked those of the giant, fierce beast known as the Hydra of Lerna fought by Hercules in Greek mythology. The Hydra of Lerna was a many-headed sea serpent that grew a new head each time one of its existing heads was lopped off by a swordsman.

When Trembley cut a hydra in two, he found it possessed the ability to regenerate itself—to grow back the parts he cut off. Trembley also saw that the pieces he cut off grew their own heads and tentacles.

Although Trembley made many observations of the hydra, he did not know why the animal was able to regenerate its organs and other body parts. More than two centuries later, scientists determined that the hydra's body deployed stem cells to repair its damaged organs.

ORGAN REGENERATION

On March 9, 2009, President Barack Obama lifted the ban on using federal money to fund embryonic stem cell research. This policy change devoted billions of dollars to the research. Until then, most embryonic stem cell research had been financed with private funds. This decision will expand embryonic stem cell research, including projects that are devoted to organ regeneration.

Some studies have indicated that physicians will one day be able to coax human stem cells into forming complete organs. Already, scientists at Newcastle University in Great Britain have successfully created a tiny human liver—about the size of a coin—using stem cells. The researchers believe they are still some 15 years away from creating a full-size human liver from stem cells. Nevertheless, they see great promise in the research.

Other stem cell therapies concentrate on repairing the damaged organs before a transplant is necessary. In Fort Myers, Florida, 60-year-old Robert Pleva was able to come off the heart transplant waiting list after doctors repaired his defective heart with stem cells. "This was a case where the patient's only option for survival was heart

Sally Essex donated a portion of her healthy liver to John Tomlin, a liver cancer patient. Parts of livers can grow into whole, healthy livers.

transplant, and that is no longer the case," said cardiologist Zannos Grekos, who headed the team that developed Pleva's therapy. "We couldn't be more pleased with this outcome."[4]

Pleva was not treated with embryonic stem cells but so-called adult stem cells. Like embryonic stem cells, adult stem cells are undifferentiated. They are found in the organs, tissue, and fluids of adults and children. They can be withdrawn, nurtured, and returned to the patient's body, where they can be coaxed into repairing damaged organs and other body parts.

Embryonic stem cells may have different potential from adult stem cells, because they can become almost any cell type. Opponents of embryonic stem cell therapy see great promise in adult stem cell research. Many have called for all funding for embryonic stem cell research to be dropped, but some scientists insist that both therapies should be pursued because each type has unique possibilities.

The Future of Artificial Organs

While researchers pursue stem cell therapies, others have concentrated on replacing damaged organs with artificial organs. The history of artificial organs dates back to 1944. Dutch physician Willem Kolff

The First Dialysis Patient

The dialysis machine filters impurities out of the blood of patients whose kidneys have failed. Physician Willem Kolff's first 16 patients died, but his seventeenth patient lived for seven years on artificial dialysis. The patient was a woman who had collaborated with the Nazis during the German occupation of Holland. After World War II, Kolff's decision to save her life was met with anger. "People begged, 'Let her die,'" Kolff said years later. "But no physician has the right to decide whether a patient is a good guy or not. He must treat every patient who has need of him."[5] Kolff died in 2009 at the age of 97.

invented the dialysis machine, which performs the functions of the kidney. Two to three times a week, a patient must spend several hours hooked to the large machine as it removes waste from the blood. Although newer, compact machines can be used at home, designers have not been able to create a dialysis device that can be implanted in the body.

However, producing a small, compact, and implantable heart is a breakthrough that some scientists believe is attainable. The original artificial heart was also a huge device. The power pack that operated the mechanical organ had to be wheeled around behind the patient in a shopping cart. The first patient, Barney Clark, received the implant on December 2, 1982. He lived for 112 days. Today, artificial hearts have been greatly reduced in size but are still regarded as experimental devices. Many designs are under development. Researchers hope that, within the next decade, artificial hearts may become at least temporary replacements for diseased human hearts.

A Multifaceted Issue

Until artificial organs are perfected or stem cell research shows significant results, many people find themselves wrestling with the moral issues involved in organ donation. Some people's religions permit them to donate their organs or even encourage them to do so, but other religions forbid it. Some people feel uncomfortable ending the life-sustaining measures for their comatose loved ones. Some find the idea of a deceased mother, father, family member, or stranger providing organs and other body parts morbid. Others, including lawmakers, argue over the idea of legalizing a trade in organs in order to regulate it. Some states have already passed laws that compensate donors for the costs associated with organ donation. Others argue that organ donors should never receive payment for giving a part of their bodies.

Meanwhile, most people in need of new organs have no choice but to remain on long waiting lists.

What Is Xenotransplantation?

Xenotransplantation is a procedure that uses an organ provided by an animal to temporarily replace a human organ until a suitable donor organ is found. Experiments with xenotransplantation have been ongoing for more than 25 years.

The attempts to perform the transplants have largely met with failure, mostly because of the human body's tendency to reject the animal organs. The most celebrated case on record occurred in 1984 when a young girl, known as "Baby Fae," was born with a defective heart. With no donor heart immediately available, doctors transplanted the heart of a baboon into the baby. A week after the transplant, Baby Fae's immune system rejected the heart and the child died.

For many, the wait ends in tragic consequences as they find themselves overcome with disease before replacement organs are available. With medical advances and the generosity of others, many people do receive organs, though, and go on to live active lives. ⌒

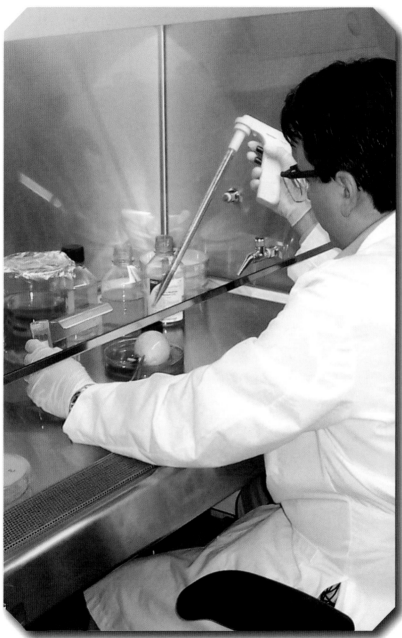

Scientists research ways in which human organs can be regrown from tissue samples.

Timeline

200 CE	1740	1774
Hua-Tuo, a Chinese surgeon, suggests transplanted organs could replace diseased organs.	Swiss naturalist Abraham Trembley observes the powers of organ regeneration in a tiny pond animal that he names the hydra.	William Hewson, a physician who taught medical students anatomy by dissecting bodies in a London basement, dies of blood poisoning.

1906	1944	1954
Christian Science founder Mary Baker Eddy publishes *Science and Health*. It suggests that faith in God can cure diseases of the organs.	Dutch physician Willem Kolff develops the kidney dialysis machine.	Doctors perform the first kidney transplant on a human patient.

1816

Mary Wollstonecraft Shelley writes *Frankenstein*, a novel in which cadaver organs are transplanted to sustain life.

1832

Britain adopts the Anatomy Act. People can donate the bodies of their deceased loved ones to science.

1905

On December 7, Eduard Zirm performs the first cornea transplant.

1963

A patient in Mississippi undergoes the first lung transplant; doctors perform the first liver transplant.

1966

A patient in Minnesota receives the first transplanted pancreas.

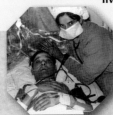

1967

On December 3, South African Louis Washkansky receives the first heart transplant; he lives for 18 days.

TIMELINE

1968

Leaders of the medical community convene a symposium to develop a clear definition of death.

1982

On December 2, Barney Clark receives the first artificial heart; he survives for 112 days.

1984

Congress establishes the Organ Procurement and Transportation Network to match patients with donor organs.

1999

Doctors in Belgium perform a bloodless kidney transplant on a member of the Jehovah's Witnesses faith.

2002

On February 16, liver-transplant recipient and snowboarder Chris Klug wins a bronze medal at the Winter Olympics.

2004

President George W. Bush signs legislation to provide live donors with financial assistance to help pay their expenses.

1993	1994	1995
Pennsylvania Governor Robert P. Casey receives a new heart and liver a day after he was placed on the waiting list for the organs.	The American Medical Association finds it acceptable to begin harvesting the organs of anencephalic infants before their deaths.	Mickey Mantle receives a liver transplant one day after his name was entered in the national database.

2006	2008	2009
China enacts a law outlawing the sale of organs harvested from condemned prisoners.	Michael Mastromarino is sentenced to at least 18 years in prison for illegally harvesting skin and body parts.	On March 9, President Barack Obama lifts restrictions on federal funding for embryonic stem cell research.

ESSENTIAL FACTS

AT ISSUE

Opposed

❖ Doctors, bioethicists, and others have struggled with the definition of death. Many doctors oppose harvesting organs until the heart and lungs have stopped on their own. Even then, it is unclear how much time the organs should be given to see if they resume functioning.

❖ Some bioethicists question the procedures that cool the organs before the donor has died, believing the activity begins the harvesting process while the patient still has the opportunity to recover.

❖ Some faiths oppose the procedures involved in organ donation.

❖ Some people oppose a legal organ trade because of moral reservations about selling body parts. They also worry that poor people will be preyed upon.

In Favor

❖ Transplanted hearts, livers, kidneys, pancreases, and other organs from deceased people have saved many lives. In the case of kidneys, the donors can be living.

❖ Many religions endorse organ donation, finding it to be an act of charity.

❖ Bodies donated to science enable medical students to learn anatomy by dissecting cadavers. Also, research scientists and biotechnology companies can develop new drugs and medical techniques by experimenting on donated body parts.

❖ Some believe a legal organ trade will help establish safer and more regulated procedures for selling and buying organs. Paying organ donors will likely increase the amount of organs available.

CRITICAL DATES

December 7, 1905
Austrian ophthalmologist Eduard Zirm successfully transplanted the cornea of an eye. A century later, U.S. doctors perform 40,000 cornea transplants a year.

December 3, 1967
South African surgeon Christiaan Barnard performed the first heart transplant on Louis Washkansky, a Cape Town grocery store owner. Washkansky survived for 18 days.

1968
Leaders of the medical community convened a symposium at Harvard University to resolve the definition of death. Their efforts were aimed at preventing organ harvesting from live donors and eventually resulted in the Uniform Determination of Death Act, which has been adopted by all 50 states and the District of Columbia.

April 5, 2004
President George W. Bush signed the Organ Donation and Recovery Improvement Act. This made federal financial assistance available to kidney donors to help them with expenses they incur as a result of their surgeries.

QUOTES

"When I first heard that I would die if they couldn't get me a liver within two years, I thought no problem. But then I found out the odds might not be so good. And it doesn't make any sense. If everyone agreed to organ donation, there wouldn't be any list at all."—*Walter Payton, Hall of Fame football player who died of liver failure in 1999*

"The image this creates is people hovering over the body trying to get organs any way they can. There's a kind of macabre flavor to it."—*Michael A. Grodin, director of bioethics at Boston University, commenting on the need to remove organs soon after death occurs*

ADDITIONAL RESOURCES

SELECT BIBLIOGRAPHY

Altman, Lawrence K. "Christiaan Barnard, 78, Surgeon for First Heart Transplant, Dies." *New York Times*. 3 Sept. 2001. 22 June 2009 <http://www.nytimes.com/2001/09/03/world/christiaan-barnard-78-surgeon-for-first-heart-transplant-dies.html>.

Kolata, Gina. "Transplants, Morality and Mickey." *New York Times*. 11 June 1995. 22 June 2009 <http://www.nytimes.com/1995/06/11/weekinreview/the-nation-transplants-morality-and-mickey.html>.

Tilney, Nicholas L. *Transplants: From Myth to Reality*. New Haven, CT: Yale University Press, 2003.

Veatch, Robert M. *Transplantation Ethics*. Washington DC: Georgetown University Press, 2000.

FURTHER READING

Ballard, Carol. *Organ Transplants*. Chicago, IL: World Almanac Library, 2007.

Barter, James. *Great Medical Discoveries—Organ Transplants*. San Diego, CA: Lucent, 2005.

Klug, Chris, and Steve Jackson. *To the Edge and Back: My Story from Organ Transplant Survivor to Olympic Snowboarder*. New York, NY: Carroll & Graf, 2004.

Macdonald, Helen. *Human Remains: Dissection and Its Histories*. New Haven, CT: Yale University Press, 2006.

WEB LINKS

To learn more about organ and body donation, visit ABDO Publishing Company online at **www.abdopublishing.com**. Web sites about organ and body donation are featured on our Book Links page. These links are routinely monitored and updated to provide the most current information available.

FOR MORE INFORMATION

For more information on this subject, contact or visit the following organizations.

The Franklin Institute
222 North Twentieth Street, Philadelphia, PA 19103
215-448-1200
www2.fi.edu
The museum displays the world's largest facsimile of a human heart, which is large enough for visitors to walk through. Visitors can participate in many interactive exhibits associated with the display, including a mock-up of a surgical theater where they can watch a virtual patient undergo heart surgery.

National Museum of American History, Smithsonian Institution
Fourteenth Street and Constitution Avenue Northwest
Washington, DC 20560
202-357-2145
www.americanhistory.si.edu
The museum's collection includes a display of more than 150 artificial organs, including several versions of artificial hearts. The artificial organ exhibit is part of a collection that includes more than 80,000 objects associated with medical science.

Warren Anatomical Museum
Countway Library of Medicine, Center for the History of Medicine, Harvard University, 10 Shattuck Street, Boston, MA 02115
617-432-6196
www.countway.harvard.edu/menuNavigation/historicalResources/warrenAnatomicalMuseum.html
The Warren Anatomical Museum was created from a collection of medical specimens left to the university by physician John Collins Warren, who died in 1856. Warren compiled some 15,000 specimens of organs and other body parts as well as photographs and instruments, many of which are on display at the museum.

Glossary

adult stem cells
Cells found in the blood and tissue of children and adults that have not yet formed into the cells for organs or other components of the body.

antirejection drugs
Drugs that fight the rejection of a donor organ by the body's immune system.

bioethicists
Professionals who study the ethical and moral implications of health and medical procedures.

blastocysts
The very young embryos, consisting of just a few hundred cells, that form after conception; blastocysts contain embryonic stem cells.

blood transfusions
The medical procedures that supply blood from donors to another person.

brain-dead
The physical condition in which electrical activity in the brain has ceased.

cardiac arrest
A condition in which the heart abruptly stops beating.

cirrhosis
A scarring of the liver, which impedes blood flow through the organ, often resulting in organ failure.

diabetes
A disease that results when the pancreas fails to produce the chemical insulin, causing a buildup of sugar in the blood.

dialysis machine
A device that performs the functions of the kidneys by cleaning impurities from the patient's blood.

embryonic stem cell
A very young cell found in an embryo known as a blastocyst. It has the potential to turn into many other types of cells.

end-stage renal disease
>The final stage of kidney disease when the kidneys near failure.

fundamentalist Christians
>Christians who believe in a literal interpretation of the Bible, meaning they believe the Scriptures are true, word for word.

hepatitis
>A disease transmitted through blood that causes an inflammation of the liver and, in many cases, liver failure.

hypertension
>Also known as high blood pressure, a condition that causes the heart to work harder to pump blood.

insulin
>A chemical manufactured by the pancreas that controls the level of sugar in the blood.

in vitro fertilization
>The procedure in which a mother's egg is fertilized with the father's sperm in a laboratory dish. The fertilized egg is then surgically returned to the womb, where it develops into a fetus.

living wills
>Legal documents in which people provide instructions about whether they want life-sustaining machines turned off should they be permanently incapacitated by a disease or an accident.

necrosis
>A disease that causes the death of tissue.

organ harvesting
>The procedure to remove organs, tissue, and other components from cadavers.

traumatic brain injury
>Any injury sustained by the head that disrupts brain functions.

xenotransplantation
>The medical procedure that implants an organ from an animal into the human body.

SOURCE NOTES

Chapter 1. Overcoming the Odds

1. Edward Wong. "Defying the Odds Again, Klug Grabs the Bronze." *New York Times*. 16 Feb. 2002. D-1.

2. Wayne Drehs. "Family of Walter Payton Works to Increase Organ Donor Awareness." *ESPN.com*. 22 Feb. 2008. 6 July 2009 <http://sports.espn.go.com/espn/blackhistory2008/news/story?id=3258762>.

3. "Two Families Make One Dream a Reality." *ESPN.com*. 10 Feb. 2002. 29 July 2009 <http://sports.espn.go.com/oly/winter02/gen/story?id=1326699>.

4. "About CKF." *Chris Klug Foundation*. 29 July 2009 <http://chrisklugfoundation.org/about-ckf.html>.

5. "Living Liver Donor Who Saved Life of Mother-In-Law Represents Cedars-Sinai in Rose Parade." *Medical News Today*. 2 Jan. 2007. 6 July 2009 <www.medicalnewstoday.com/articles/59868.php>.

6. "Meet Team Transplant." *American Transplant Foundation*. 29 July 2009 <http://www.americantransplantfoundation.org/teamtransplant.htm>.

Chapter 2. History of Donation

1. Christopher Goulding. "The Real Dr. Frankenstein?" *Journal of the Royal Society of Medicine*. May 2002. 258.

2. Mary Shelley. *Frankenstein*. Boston, MA: Bedford/St. Martin's, 2000. 58–59.

3. Lawrence K. Altman. "Christiaan Barnard, 78, Surgeon for First Heart Transplant, Dies." *New York Times*. 3 Sept. 2001. A-1.

4. Margaret M. Lock. *Twice Dead*. Berkeley, CA: University of California Press, 2002. 84.

Chapter 3. Defining Death

1. Alexander Morgan Capron. "Harvesting Organs From Anencephalic Infants." *Headline News-Science News*. Washington DC: National Academy Press, 1991. 189.

2. National Conference of Commissioners of Uniform State Laws. "Uniform Determination of Death Act." 26 July–1 Aug. 1980. 6 July 2009 <http://www.law.upenn.edu/bll/archives/ulc/fnact99/1980s/udda80.htm>.

3. Rob Stein. "New Trend in Organ Donation Raises Questions." *Washington Post*. 18 March 2007. A-3.

4. Ibid.

Chapter 4. Organs for Transplant

1. Richard Deitsch. "Q&A Everson Walls." *SportsIllustrated.com*. 31 Dec. 2007. 29 July 2009 <http://vault.sportsillustrated.cnn.com/vault/article/magazine/MAG1115157/index.htm>.

2. Adam Duerson. "Spare A Cerebellum?" *Sports Illustrated*. 6 Oct. 2008. 20.

3. Ronald Munson. *Raising the Dead: Organ Transplants, Ethics, and Society*. New York, NY: Oxford University Press, 2002. 5.

4. Marrecca Fiore. "How to Donate Your Body to Science." *Fox News Online*. 13 June 2007. 6 July 2009 <http://www.foxnews.com/story/0,2933,281793,00.html>.

5. Nicholas L. Tilney. *Transplants: From Myth to Reality*. New Haven, CT: Yale University Press, 2003. 184.

Chapter 5. Organ Recipients

1. "Prisoner Gets $1M Heart Transplant." *CBSnews.com*. 31 Jan. 2002. 29 July 2009 <http://www.cbsnews.com/stories/2002/01/31/health/main326305.shtml>.

2. Ruthann Richter. "Local Transplant Patient and Wife Reach Out to Inmate Who Received New Heart." *Stanford Report*. 6 Feb. 2002. 6 July 2009 <http://news.stanford.edu/news/2002/february6/transplant.html>.

3. Ibid.

4. Robert M. Veatch. *Transplantation Ethics*. Washington DC: Georgetown University Press, 2000. 356.

5. Allen R. Myerson. "Mantle Receives New Liver As Donor Is Found Quickly." *New York Times Online*. 9 June 1995. 3 Aug. 2009 <http://www.nytimes.com/1995/06/09/sports/mantle-receives-new-liver-as-donor-is-found-quickly.html>.

6. Gina Kolata. "Transplants, Morality and Mickey." *New York Times*. 11 June 1995. 4–5.

7. "Sports People: Baseball; Mantles Unveil Organ Donor Program." *New York Times Online*. 18 Aug. 1995. 3 Aug. 2009 <http://www.nytimes.com/1995/08/18/sports/sports-people-baseball-mantles-unveil-organ-donor-program.html>.

Source Notes Continued

Chapter 6. Organ Donors

1. "Americans Register Importance of Organ Donation." *Reuters Online*. 7 June 2007. 6 July 2009 <http://www.reuters.com/article/lifestyleMolt/idUSN0645054320070607>.

2. "Liver Transplant for Jehovah's Witness." *BBC News Online*. 14 May 1999. 6 July 2009 <http://news.bbc.co.uk/2/hi/health/342927.stm>.

3. "Pope To Group On Organ Transplants: New Way Of Sharing Life With Others." *Priests for Life*. 20 June 1991. 3 Aug. 2009 <http://www.priestsforlife.org/magisterium/91-06-20popeorgantransplant.htm>.

4. Brad Harrub. "A Christian's Response to Organ Donation and Transplantation." *Apologetics Press*. 2003. 6 July 2009 <http://www.apologeticspress.org/articles/2164>.

5. Ibid.

Chapter 7. Transplant Tourism

1. Sadaqat Jan. "Poor Pakistanis Donate Kidneys for Money." *Washington Post*. 12 Nov. 2006. 6 July 2009 <http://www.washingtonpost.com/wp-dyn/content/article/2006/11/12/AR2006111200375.html>.

2. Anuj Chopra. "India's Black Market Racket in Human Kidneys." *U.S. News Online*. 1 Feb. 2008. 3 Aug. 2009 <http://www.usnews.com/articles/news/world/2008/02/01/indias-black-market-racket-in-human-kidneys.html>.

3. "Bills Regulating Organ Donation And Transplantation Discussed." *House of Representatives, Philippines*. 29 Apr. 2009. 3 Aug. 2009 <http://www.congress.gov.ph/committees/commnews/commnews_det.php?newsid=1122>.

4. Calum McLeod. "China Makes Ultimate Punishment Mobile." *USA Today Online*. 15 June 2006. 6 July 2009 <http://www.usatoday.com/news/world/2006-06-14-death-van_x.htm>.

5. Nancy Scheper-Hughes. "The New Cannibalism." *New Internationalist*. 3 Aug. 2009 <http://www.newint.org/issue300/trade.html>.

6. Scott Carney. "Why a Kidney (Street Value: $3,000) Sells for $85,000." *Wired*. 8 May 2007. 6 July 2009 <http://www.wired.com/medtech/health/news/2007/05/india_transplants_prices>.

Chapter 8. Compensation for Donors
1. Michele Goodwin. "The Organ Donor Taboo." *Forbes Online*. 15 Oct. 2007. 6 July 2009 <http://www.forbes.com/forbes/2007/1015/032.html>.
2. Richard Knox. "Should We Legalize the Market for Human Organs?" *National Public Radio Online*. 21 May 2008. 6 July 2009 <http://www.npr.org/templates/story/story.php?storyId=90632108>.
3. Jeneen Interlandi. "Not Just Urban Legend." *Newsweek Online*. 10 Jan. 2009. 6 July 2009 <http://www.newsweek.com/id/178873>.
4. "House of Commons Debates, Organ Donation (Presumed Consent) Bill." *They Work for You*. 13 Mar. 2009. 6 July 2009 <http://www.theyworkforyou.com/debates/?id=2009-03-13a.609.0>.
5. Ibid.
6. Jeneen Interlandi. "Not Just Urban Legend." *Newsweek Online*. 10 Jan. 2009. 6 July 2009 <http://www.newsweek.com/id/178873>.
7. Richard Knox. "Should We Legalize the Market for Human Organs?" *National Public Radio Online*. 21 May 2008. 6 July 2009 <http://www.npr.org/templates/story/story.php?storyId=90632108>.
8. Stephen J. Dubner and Steven D. Levitt. "Flesh Trade: Why Not Let People Sell Their Organs?" *New York Times Magazine*. 9 July 2006. 20.

Chapter 9. Alternatives to Organ Donation
1. Eve Herold. "Stem Cells and the New Future of Medicine." *USA Today/Findarticles*. Mar. 2003. 3 Aug. 2009 <http://findarticles.com/p/articles/mi_m1272/is_2694_131/ai_98829811/>.
2. Ibid.
3. Judie Brown. "We Deserve Better Than Stem Cell Research Fraud." *American Life League*. 10 Jan. 2007. 6 July 2009 <http://www.all.org/article.php?id=10907>.
4. "Regenocyte Therapeutic Reports Successful Treatment of Cardiomyopathy with Stem Cells." *Pipeline Review*. 10 Feb. 2009. 6 July 2009 <http://www.pipelinereview.com/index.php/2009021125170/DNA-RNA-and-Cells/Regenocyte-Therapeutic-Reports-Successful-Treatment-of-Cardiomyopathy-with-Stem-Cell.html>.
5. David Brown. "Doctor Invented Kidney Dialysis Machine, Artificial Organs." *Washington Post*. 13 Feb. 2009. B7.

INDEX

ABOUT THE AUTHOR

Hal Marcovitz is a former newspaper reporter who has written more than 130 books for young readers. As a newspaper reporter, he was the recipient of three Keystone Press Awards, the highest award for journalism presented by the Pennsylvania Newspaper Association. *Nancy Pelosi*, his 2005 biography of House Speaker Nancy Pelosi, was named to *Booklist* magazine's list of recommended feminist books for young readers. He makes his home in Chalfont, Pennsylvania, with his wife and daughter.

PHOTO CREDITS